W9-BXH-475

The Let's Talk Library™

Let's Talk About
Going to the Doctor

Marianne Johnston

The Rosen Publishing Group's

PowerKids Press™

New York

HP BR
J
RJ50.5
.J64
1997

Published in 1997 by The Rosen Publishing Group, Inc.
29 East 21st Street, New York, NY 10010

Copyright © 1997 by The Rosen Publishing Group, Inc.

All rights reserved. No part of this book may be reproduced in any form without permission in writing from the publisher, except by a reviewer.

First Edition

Book design: Erin McKenna

Photo credits: All photos by Seth Dinnerman.

Johnston, Marianne.
    Let's talk about going to the doctor / Marianne Johnston.
        p.   cm. — (The Let's talk library)
    Includes index.
    Summary: Explains what happens during a typical visit to the doctor, covering such activities as having your temperature taken, having your blood pressure measured, and getting a shot.
    ISBN 0-8239-5035-2
    1. Children—Medical examinations—Juvenile literature. 2. Children—Preparation for medical care—Juvenile literature. [1. Medical care.] I. Title. II. Series.
RJ50.5.J64 1996
610—dc20   96-27205
                                                                        CIP
                                                                          AC

Manufactured in the United States of America

Table of Contents

What Is a Doctor?

A **doctor** (DOK-ter) is someone who keeps people healthy. A **pediatrician** (pee-dee-uh-TRIH-shun) is a doctor who only takes care of kids. One way she does this is by giving them check-ups at least once a year. Sometimes you don't know that you're sick. A doctor can tell. She will make sure that you stay as healthy as possible. You may be so sick that you can't get better without some help. Mom or Dad may take you to the pediatrician. She will make sure you get the **medicine** (MED-ih-sin) you need to get well.

◀ A doctor can help make sure that you are healthy so you can do the things you want to do.

The Waiting Room

When you first get to the doctor's office, you will have to wait in a waiting room. Your parents may have to fill out some forms. But you can read the magazines or books or play with the toys that are in the waiting room. You can also bring your own toys or books.

Before you see the doctor, you'll see a nurse. She calls your name when she's ready to see you. Your mom or dad can stay with you for the entire checkup.

Reading or playing with toys makes the ▶
time in the waiting room go by faster.

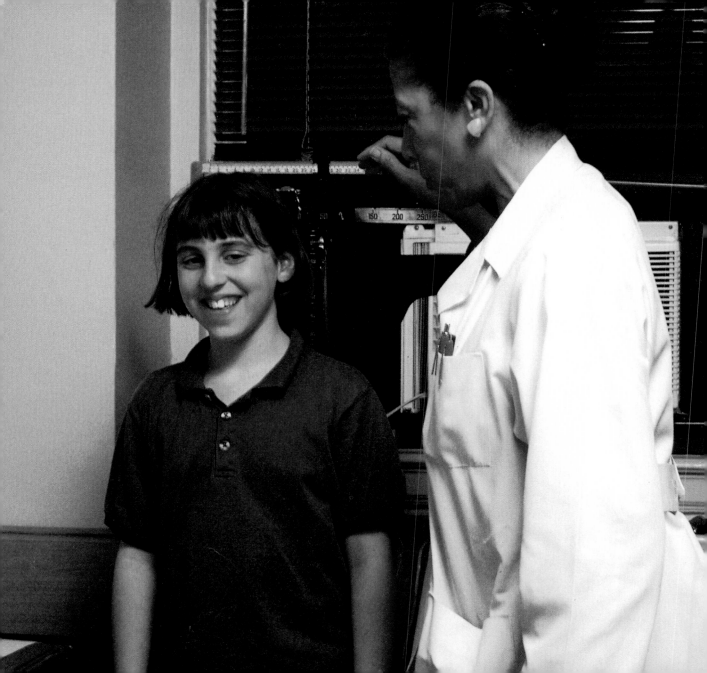

Before You See the Doctor

First, the nurse weighs you on the scale. Your weight helps tell the doctor if you're growing the way you should. Then she takes your **blood pressure** (BLUD PREH-sher) to make sure your heart is pumping blood through your body the right way. The nurse will probably take your **temperature** (TEM-prah-cher), too. This is to make sure your body isn't too hot or too cold.

Then you get to see the doctor.

◀ Many scales that measure your weight have a special ruler for measuring how tall you are.

The Examination Room

The doctor gives you your checkup in the **examination** (eg-zam-in-AY-shun) room. The examining table is in the middle of the room. This is where you sit during your checkup. There is also a sink and a tray with all of the doctor's **instruments** (IN-struh-mints) on it. The doctor uses these to examine you. Many examination rooms have neat posters that show how the body works. Some even show you what kinds of foods you should eat to stay healthy.

There are lots of interesting things to look at in the doctor's office. ▶

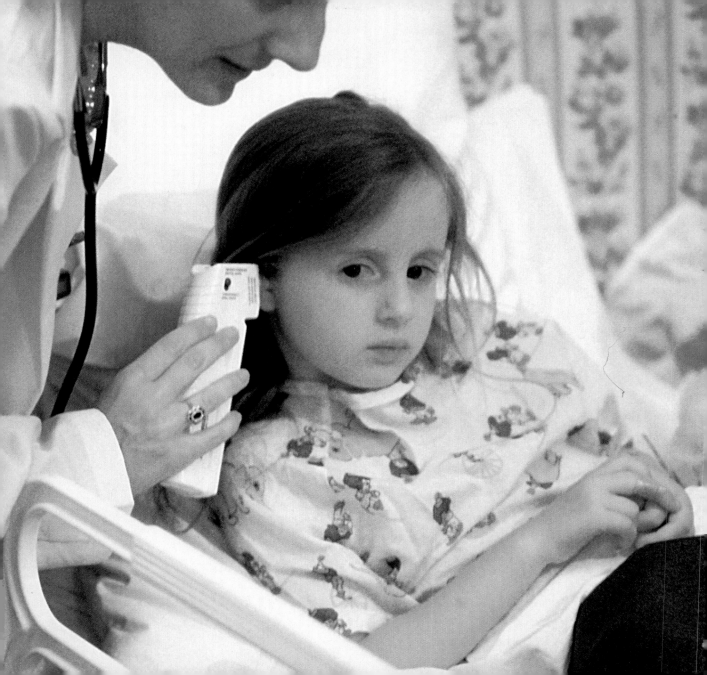

The Checkup

At the beginning of the checkup the doctor asks you to take off your clothes. But you can leave your underwear on. Then the doctor examines you. She checks out each part of your body. She'll listen to your heartbeat and to your breathing. She'll check your ears, nose, and throat. When she checks your throat, she'll ask you to open your mouth and say, "Aaah." The doctor will also take a good look at your spine to make sure it is straight. Then she'll ask you how you've been feeling.

◀ The doctor checks each part of your body to make sure you are healthy.

13

A Doctor's Instruments

The doctor uses different instruments to examine you. A **stethoscope** (STETH-uh-scope) lets him listen to your lungs and your heart. He uses an **otoscope** (AH-toe-scope) to look inside your ears and nose and down your throat. An otoscope looks like a big pen with a light on the end. The doctor also uses a **tongue depressor** (TUNG dee-PRESS-er) to look at your throat and mouth. A tongue depressor looks like a big Popsicle stick. It doesn't hurt when he uses these instruments. They just help him check your body better.

The stethoscope helps the doctor listen to your breathing and your heartbeat. ▶

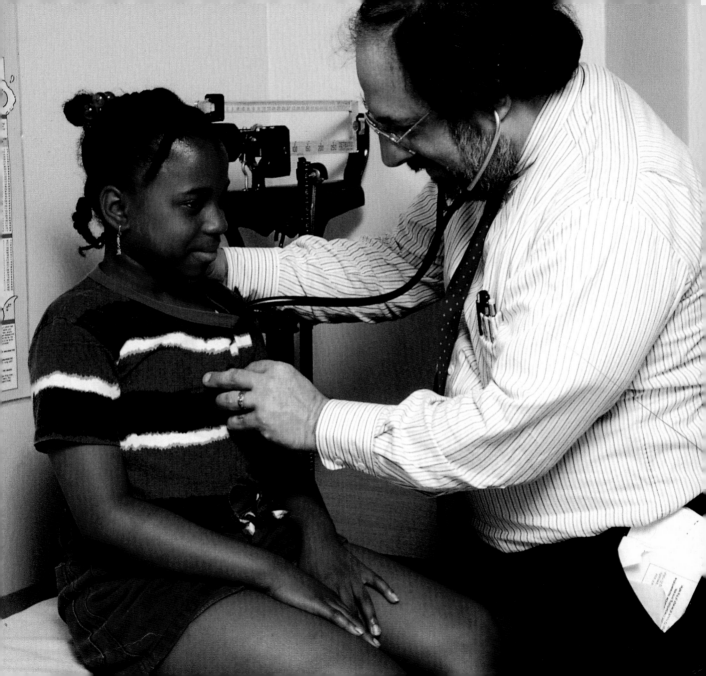

Tests

Doctors also need to find out what's happening on the inside of your body. One way to do this is to examine your **urine** (YUR-in). The nurse gives you a plastic cup. You go into the bathroom and urinate into it.

Then the nurse checks your urine to make sure you are healthy. It may seem **weird** (WEERD), but doctors can tell a lot about what's happening inside you from your urine.

◀ Everybody has to give a urine sample.

Shots

You may need to get a shot while you're at the doctor's office. These shots are **vaccinations** (vak-sin-AY-shunz). A vaccination is a special shot that keeps you from getting certain **diseases** (dih-ZEEZ-ez). The doctor uses a needle to give you the shot in your arm. It may feel like a pinch. Your arm may be a little sore afterward. But the soreness goes away. Then you can be sure you will not get that disease.

Vaccinations keep you safe from many diseases. ▶

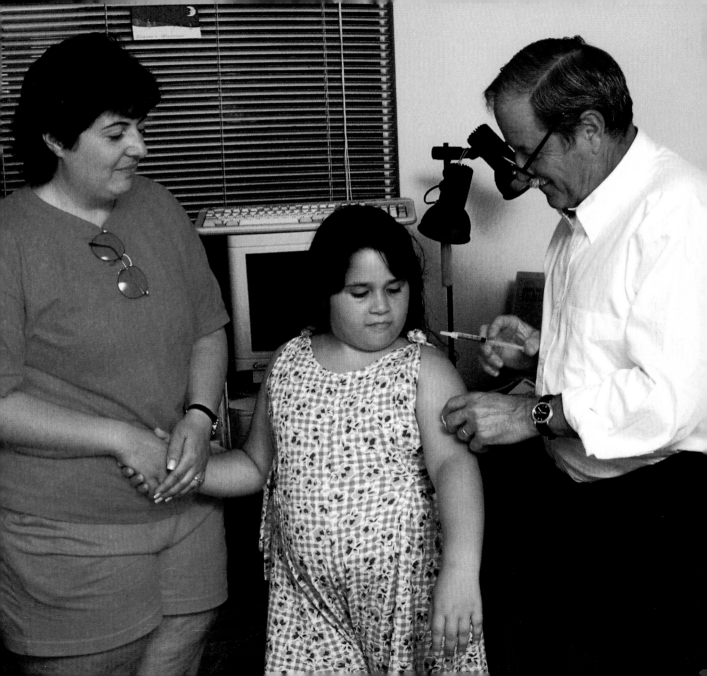

The Pharmacist

If you're sick, the doctor may say that you need medicine. The doctor writes out a **prescription** (preh-SKRIP-shun) for the medicine. The prescription explains the type of medicine you need. It also tells you how often you should take it. Your mom or dad takes the prescription to the **pharmacist** (FAR-muh-sist). A pharmacist knows all about different medicines. He or she gives the prescription to your mom or dad. Then your mom or dad gives you the medicine until the medicine is gone.

◄ If you need special medicine, the doctor writes out a prescription for it.

Asking Questions

When you visit the doctor you may not understand everything that happens. The doctor uses instruments that you may not have seen before. The doctor may ask you to do funny things such as cough, breathe deeply, or walk in a straight line. Don't be afraid to ask about anything that the doctor says or does. The doctor will take the time to explain what she is doing and why. She wants you to feel comfortable during your visit. But most of all, she wants to help keep you happy and healthy.

Glossary

blood pressure (BLUD PREH-sher) The pressure created by your heart pumping blood through your body.

disease (dih-ZEEZ) Sickness.

doctor (DOK-ter) Person who is trained to treat sickness.

examination (eg-zam-in-AY-shun) Looking at something or someone closely and carefully.

instrument (IN-struh-mint) Tool.

medicine (MED-ih-sin) Something used to treat a sickness or a disease.

otoscope (AH-toe-scope) Instrument used to examine a person's ears, nose, and throat.

pediatrician (pee-dee-uh-TRIH-shun) Doctor who only takes care of kids.

pharmacist (FAR-muh-sist) Person who is trained to make medicine.

prescription (preh-SKRIP-shun) Written order for making and using a medicine.

stethoscope (STETH-uh-scope) Instrument used to listen to a person's lungs and heart.

temperature (TEM-prah-cher) Degree of heat or cold.

tongue depressor (TUNG dee-PRESS-er) Wooden stick used to hold down the tongue while the doctor examines a person's throat.

urine (YUR-in) Bodily waste; pee.

vaccination (vak-sin-AY-shun) A shot that helps protect a person from a disease.

weird (WEERD) Strange; odd.

Index

4/06

BOSTON PUBLIC LIBRARY

3 9999 03554 998 7